Still All Scrapped Out!

More ideas for taming your unruly collection of scraps.

Happy Quilting!
Penni Domikis
2013

by Penni Domikis

www.cabininthewoodsquilters.com

CONTENTS

©2012 Penni Domikis for Cabin In The Woods
Quilters

Developmental Editor: Penni Domikis
Cover Designs: Cabin Digital
Book Design: Cabin Digital
Illustrator: Cabin Digital
Photography: Cabin Digital
Machine Quilting: Elizabeth Bigger
  (Liz B Quilting)
Editor: Jennifer Plaugher
Published by Cabin Digital
Fredericksburg, VA

Attention Teachers:
To obtain copies of this text for teaching,
you may contact Cabin In The Woods Quilters
through the website at:
www.cabininthewoodsquilters.com
or by emailing us at:
cabininthewoodsquilters@gmail.com

Still All Scrapped Out!: More ideas for making
a masterpiece from your unruly collection of
scraps.
2nd Edition: November 2013
ISBN: 978-0-9835325-3-8 (spiral pbk.)

Printed in the United States of America

ACKNOWLEDGEMENTS:
Thank you to ...
My family who puts up with long hours and
shirked responsibilities while I am elbow deep
in scraps. My wonderful friends and quilting
buddies who are endlessly supportive of me
and my creative ideas and who lecture me
on procrastination and priorities... what
true friends you are. The staff who provides
endless entertainment and distraction.

Introduction

Last year I reached a point of no return in quilting. The scraps in my studio had compounded to a near catastrophic level. I found no other solution than to dump them out and stitch them together into a string of ideas for my first book, *All Scrapped Out!* It was my goal to come up with an idea that would free my community of quilters from the perfect patchwork rules they were used to and give them permission to create a masterpiece from a mess. I told thousands of students, lecture attendees and quilt show patrons that they no longer needed to use their rulers to measure strips, press their fabrics or use foundations. I told them to sit and sew. I told them to put their scraps into a paper bag and pull out random pieces to stitch together. I told them the rules were... that there were no rules.

I am sure you can image that I looked into the faces of many confused quilters. Some quietly stared at me puzzled and said that I was crazy... that my method could not possibly work. Some claimed that they didn't have the scraps for that kind of thing. Some had no confidence in their ability or vision to put colors together the way that I had done. Some simply walked away shaking their heads claiming that I had been sniffing too much fabric.

I will agree with the last group... I do enjoy lolling in my fabric sniffing the sweet smell of acquisition, but the rest are just in need of a good talking to. I managed to convince a few with some fast talk and a salesman's smile to purchase the book or take a class and give it a try. The results were quite spectacular.

I will admit that a few of my students attended class with scraps that had clearly been pre-sorted in colors. One student chose to bring only cream scraps and green scraps virtually assuring that her project, which she was sure would be a disaster, would be appealing to someone who loved the color green. One student nearly hyperventilated when after 20 minutes of confusion over which scraps to put together I placed them all into a paperbag, stirred them up and directed her to pull one out without looking and sew it to the next. One shop owner, who sat in on a class at her store, was so disturbed by the out-of-her-box process that she insisted that I at least allow her to press her scraps before she sewed them to prevent personal long term psychological damage. We quilters sure are a dramatic bunch.

I am please to announce that as of the press date of this book I know of no former student who has irreversable damage caused by my methods. I also know of no quilter who has completely abandoned their perfect patchwork forever. However, I have met many quilters who have enjoyed playing fast and loose with my rules. I love seeing the smiles of the students who are talking and laughing with their friends as they sew without care of making a mistake. I love the feeling of relief I see in a quilter's eyes when they tentatively lay their blocks out on the floor or design wall and fall in love with their quilt top. I am always thrilled to witness a student completely enveloped in the creative process of laying out the design and changing it to meet their needs... empowered to create their own masterpiece.

I couldn't have scripted the response to my book any better. I am proud and encouraged. All of you inspire me. You have certainly inspired me to come up with a few more designs that will encourage your creative process.

For those of you who are purchasing this book and are completely confused by my intended method... well... there really is no method. I did not create this book as a compilation of patterns for you to follow to the letter. This book is meant to inspire you to create a masterpiece that is one-of-a-kind and all your own. There is no pre-cutting or pre-pressing of your scraps. In essence, you will be using your scraps to create your own "fabric" from which to cut your blocks. In this book you will notice that we use lots of triangles. I know the word "triangle" in the quilting world can instantly cause panic. Never fear. We will cut the triangles in such a way that "bias", the other feared word, will not be an issue. This will free you to make quilts that you may not have otherwise tried.

The designs are actually quite simple and the quilts shown are small. I created smaller quilts in this book for the simple reason that the trunk show is just getting too big to travel. But there is no limit to the size of quilt that you can make. This is a GUIDE. Your quilt will depend on your scraps and the desired size of your finished project.

As in the first version of this book, I will provide tips for color choices and ideas at the beginning of each pattern. I will try to explain my thought process behind each design and make suggestions for you to consider when you create yours. Of course, your quilt will depend on both the desired size of your finished product and the size of the ruler that you choose to use.

There is no set ruler size for any of these projects because I want you to use the rulers that you already own. You shouldn't need to buy anything else. If you need to purchase a ruler for your project, I want you to be able to make your choice based on the type you like or the size available to you and not my requirement. The size of the ruler does not matter... as long as you use the same ruler to cut all the pieces for a single project. Of course, the size of your project will be dependent on your ruler size as well, so you may have to do a little math if you choose to make lots of changes but I have every confidence in your ability.

I sincerely hope that this book will become one of your all time favorites. May it have a treasured place on your shelf to be pulled out and dusted off whenever your scraps get a little out of control. I hope you enjoy the endless number of projects that you can create using this limitless method.

I do hope that you will continue to share your creations with me by sending me pictures of your finished masterpiece via email (cabininthewoodsquilters@gmail.com) and inviting me to visit your sewing groups and guilds. I love meeting all of you and getting together to stitch and share.

~Happy Quilting

Penni

Loving and Embracing Your Scraps

Now that you have selected this book, you should make a commitment to yourself to make something from YOUR scrap stash. So the first thing to do is get to know what you have. I was shocked when I first started thumbing through my collection. There were fabrics in there that I didn't even recognize. Then I remembered that when I was going through my "applique phase" I bought scraps from other people. I bought bags of scraps from quilt shops and quilt show booths and picked up random pieces that other people wanted to throw away. So there were lots of fabrics in those baskets that I had never used before. That was a good thing because I had many colors and patterns to choose from.

When you are selecting a project to make with your scraps you don't want to pick something that uses 5-inch squares and then find that your baskets are filled with two inch strips. I know when I began saving I chose pieces that were probably way too small to make something if I was being realistic about it. When I was organizing everything I did thin things out a bit and throw away part of my scrap stash. Most of what I threw away were corners that I cut off or little bits too small to hold. You really should go through what you have and make a decision if keeping all of it is right for you. Deciding what pieces are most useful may help you decide what to keep in the future and help keep your scraps at manageable levels.

For the purpose of this book, I filled a basket with only scrap strips. I wasn't selective about the size of the strips or the color of the strips. I just decided that anything that was between 1-inch and 6-inches wide and more than 6-inches long was a "strip" (basically, a rectangle). Once I organized all the "strips" into one basket then I started coming up with ideas to use them. You may want to keep pieces that are more square in a basket with charm squares if you like using those. I put anything that resembled small squares or triangles (and in some cases leftover pieces of blocks) into another basket to be used for something else.

If you are into Reproduction fabrics and you would like to make a scrap quilt made entirely of those then you will need to pull those pieces out of your general scraps. I found when organizing my scraps that because my reproduction quilts were often made from FQs, those scraps were much larger pieces and were better suited to store away to cut something out of later (such as parts for a sampler). The majority of those fabrics did not make it into these quilts.

In keeping with the theories from the first book, I tried to create a random project featuring pieces that may not be divided by color. One project (*Scrappy Pyramids*), uses strips from my "random florals" box. These are floral or geometric scraps that simply didn't belong with the other colors. In another project (*Delectable Diamond Scraps*), I used some other larger floral strips to create half of the block and swatches of other colors to make up the other half of the block. For all intent and purpose these scraps are random.

For the other quilts I chose to separate the scraps into color groups. There are two schools of thought when using the colored strips. You can make a block using all tones within a color group (ie. blue). This makes a much more scrappy looking project (*Scrappy Hexagons* or *Sunshine and Shadows*). The other school of thought is that you can divide those scraps into color tones (ie. powder blue, bright blue, deep navy blue, etc). Dividing the colors by tones gives you a much more planned and finished look (*From Strips to Squares, Stained Glass Lily Pads,* and *Scrappy Ozark Stars*). Sometimes when I make quilts dividing the colors by tone, viewers don't notice that the blocks are made from multiple scraps. I think this is a great compliment to the way colors can "go together" and not match.

I tried to put something for everyone in this book. It is meant to be the inspiration for your masterpiece so I really hope you will take my suggestions and run with them. The quilts in this book are much smaller than most of the designs I have done in the past to make them much easier to tote to events. You will make your quilt whatever size you want to suit your needs and your scrap stash.

Resizing Your Projects

I realize that the quilts shown in this book may be smaller than the normal desired size for your project. You may need to adjust the size of the patterns to something more suitable to you. If you want a larger quilt you will make more blocks from your scraps. I have not provided the fabric requirements in the book for the amount of scraps you will need for your quilts because they should be made from your scrap stash. It takes very few scraps of each color to make these blocks.

If you have never worked with triangles and diamonds before you may find a few of the measurements below helpful when planning your project. Here are a few of the measurements of the block sizes in the quilts that can be used to approximate the number of blocks you may need for the size project you intend to make.

Hexagons - If you cut 6-inch 60° triangles your completed hexagon blocks will measure approximately 10-inches x 12-inches.

Ozark Stars - If you cut 6-inch 60° triangles your completed Ozark Star blocks will measure approximately 22-inches x 25-inches.

Diamonds - If you cut your smaller diamonds 3-inches as directed your completed four-patch diamond blocks will measure approximately 5½-inches by 13-inches.

Selecting the Perfect Fabrics for Your Project

I know that some of you will take one look at a random fabric scrap quilt, cringe at the different fabrics within and say to yourself, "I would never make something like that." That's OK. These are your quilts and you have to make what appeals to you. However, some of us are looking for a great way to use up our stash and make something out of all the little memories of projects long forgotten. I know for me... I found strips in my stash from my first big quilt that I ever made, which I neglected to quilt properly and which will probably not make it to the next decade. So now that I know better, it's great to have a piece of my quilting history preserved in something else that might last a little longer.

Before you go about selecting your fabrics, figure out what project appeals to you the most. I tried to organize the projects by difficulty. Some of you have amazing skills with color. So you are looking at some of the more planned projects and getting some wonderful ideas. Some of us have better skills at reducing or expanding a pattern to suit our needs. The great thing about this book is that it's really designed as a jumping off point for you and your creativity. I would love to see you expand on the ideas and make it even better. You should not feel confined by this book.

If you are choosing a color organized project, you have the option of beginning by sewing your divided color strips together and figuring out a border afterwards or starting with a border fabric and choosing the tones within that border. As a rule with any scrap quilt, deep reds, browns, greens and blues tend to be great neutral colors and really allow the fabrics in the center of the quilt do the talking. In the case of *Stained Glass Hexagons*, I chose a black fabric to help those colors stand out. As you can see, it gave that quilt a whole different look.

If you choose to start with a colorful border fabric, lay all possible strips across the border fabrics and pull out any fabrics that were standing on their own. I didn't want anything to "pop out" at me. I wanted all the fabrics to blend. If you look closely you will notice that they are not necessarily all the same tones, but they do blend nicely.

Matching tones to a border fabric.

Grouping Your Assets

I find this style of quilting makes the perfect quilting bee project. If you have a group that you love to sew with, this is a really wonderful project to get your sewing group to do together. Pool your resources together to share scraps, tools and ideas.

Like many of you, I have a wonderful group of women that I like to sew with. Every group has many personalities within. There are always one or two in the group that hoard fabrics and probably have the best scraps and always one or two that buy anything and everything they can get their hands on and might have one or more of those rulers I was talking about earlier. Every group always has a least one person that is fabulous with color. She is the one that has the stash to die for and always has that perfect little piece of something that you need to complete your project. This would be the perfect time to get your sewing group together and pool your resources.

Sometimes when working on a particular project you need to concentrate really hard to keep from making a mistake and sewing something in the wrong direction. I know that I spend hours in my sewing room wishing I had my friends around me to talk to but the minute I get together with them at a retreat I get nothing done. There seems to be a breakdown between the nerve that runs my mouth and the nerve that runs the foot pedal on the sewing machine. However, the good thing about these projects is that getting started takes little concentration. You can get all the strips you need sewn to make a project in about an hour or two, and you can share all your tools and scraps and have great fun while doing it. I love teaching this technique as a workshop because the students always seem to have so much fun. Make sure you consider getting together at your friend's house or a local church or quilt shop and try this out for a day of fun with your quilting friends.

Sewing space all set to work

Using the Tools You Already Own

One of the recurring themes of this book is "using what you have." So I wanted to create designs using the tools I had lying around as well. I don't know about you, but I am fascinated with gadgets. It doesn't matter whether they are electronic or just a handy piece of plastic. I am easy prey for any quilting tool or specialty ruler on the market, as long as it makes my life easier ... and maybe makes me look like I know what I'm doing. On occasion, I purchase a ruler or tool and use it once for one quilt and it winds up in the ruler drawer. This book encourages you to get those rulers out and use them. Even if it's not listed in this book, try it out and see what you can make of it.

I used four different rulers during the making of this book: a standard square ruler (9 ½-inches or larger), a #96 Omnigrid® Triangle (90° angle x 45° angle), a Clearview™ 60° Triangle Ruler, and a Fussy Cutter™ Ruler Set 45° Diamond Guide from fast2cut™ Rulers (which makes 45° diamond shape from 1-inch to 6 ½-inches.)

- <u>Standard Square</u> - I chose to work with an Omnigrid® 9 ½-inch square ruler. I have standard squares in various sizes. This size was perfect for these projects. It was slightly larger than all my blocks but not so large as to be cumbersome. You could get away with using any square larger than this but try not to pick one so large that it's hard to maneuver on your cutting table.
- <u>#98 Omnigrid® 90°/45° Triangle Ruler</u> - I was told in a beginning quilting class that I really needed this ruler. It was one of the basic necessities of quilting. I have to admit that I have only used it once before the making of this book, not because it isn't useful, but mostly because the person who convinced me that I needed it so badly was not in my studio to show me how to use it once I brought it home. I found this ruler quite handy once I made the correlation between the size of the triangles it measured and the size of a finished square. If you have arranged quilts on point and have needed to cut setting triangles, I find that cutting them with a triangle ruler really is much easier once you get the hang of it. You can cut smaller strips that meet your needs and "flip flop" the ruler quickly. In my opinion, it creates much less waste. You can turn your square at an angle and use the 60° lines printed on it to achieve the same effect.
- <u>Clearview™ 60°Triangle Ruler 1-8-inches</u> - I bought this ruler as a specialty item to make some quilts for myself. I love making quilts with the 60° triangle because they are so easy to line up and the piecing goes together in simple rows. It can be used for kaleidoscope quilts as well. I chose to cut my blocks from the 6-inch measurement. Most of my strip sets measured just slightly larger than this ruler with approximately 3 strips per set. The Scrappy Pyramids quilt was cut from larger triangles because those strips were slightly larger. I completed the sides of the quilt the easy way by adding extra blocks and then trimming the sides square.
- <u>Fussy Cutter™ Ruler Set 45° Diamond Guide from fast2cut™ Rulers</u> - My recommendation is that you have quite a few projects under your quilter's belt before attempting to work with diamonds. The seam allowance angles can be quite challenging to wrap your head around and are definitely not for the faint of heart. If you are experienced and are ready for a challenge, you will love making *Delectable Diamond Scraps*. If you do not own this ruler and would rather not purchase it you can use the 45° printed lines on your square for this project.

Once you make a few projects from this book (and I hope you will because they are simple, quick and easy projects to make), take a glance around your sewing room/studio and look for rulers or tools that you already own that might make an interesting look when used with your strips. The best part about "playing around" with your scraps is that if you make something you don't like, you can feel comfortable throwing it out or tossing it aside without regret.

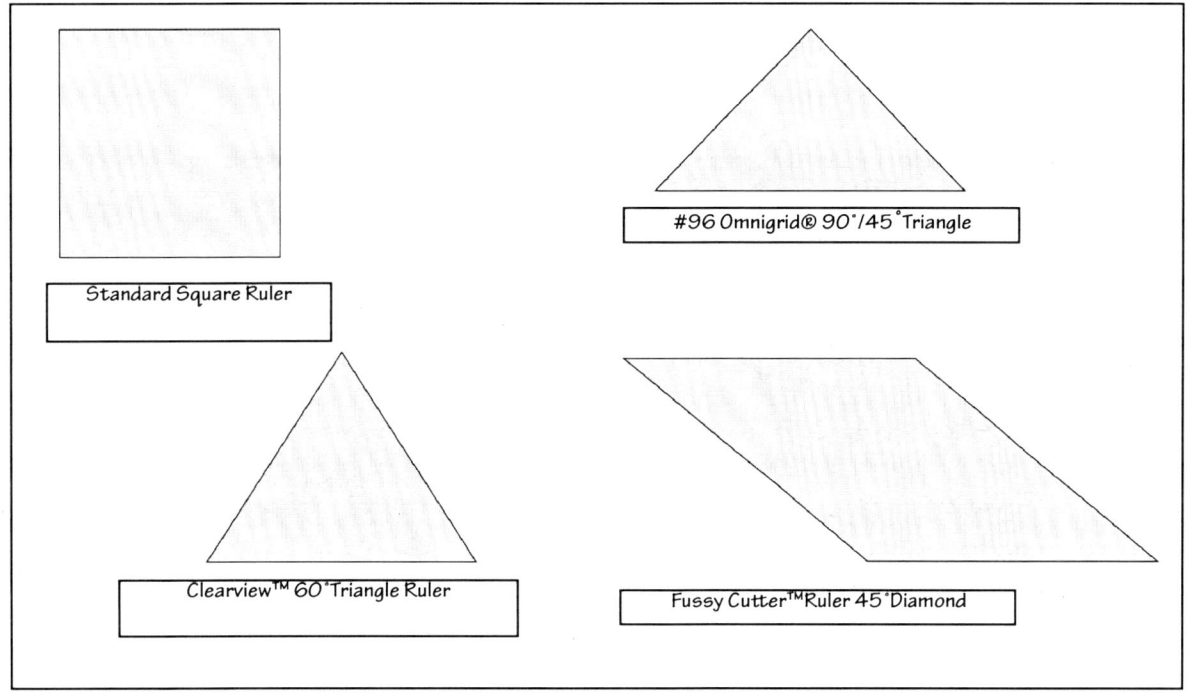

Standard Square Ruler

#96 Omnigrid® 90°/45° Triangle

Clearview™ 60° Triangle Ruler

Fussy Cutter™ Ruler 45° Diamond

Stitching Your Scraps and Making Your Blocks

Since you have read this far into the book, I suppose it's time to begin explaining how to tame these unruly scraps into something really beautiful. Be prepared. Some of you may cringe at a few things I am about to say. I understand. I have been through the same classes and have been taught the same "rules" that you have about piecing. One of the most important rules that I learned was "accuracy." If you are not accurate in your cutting and your piecing then your quilt won't turn out right. It will pucker, it won't fit together, or you will cut off valuable points and viewers will wonder about your skills.

We will bend that "accuracy" rule in this book. It's not because I don't like rules or am determined to defy authority, it's simply because those pieces that you have been saving have not been following the rules. No one told them to stay in that basket and keep their edges intact. No one told them not to fray or to get mixed up with the other sizes. So it is impossible to follow the rule of accuracy. We will eventually follow all the rules, but not during the initial piecing.

How you piece your strips together will ultimately be dictated by what quilt you have chosen to make. The quilt pattern will determine how wide or long your strip sets need to be, but we will all begin the same way. Pick up those leftover pieces and lay them out together by length. You will have some strips that will be really short (6 - 12 inches long). Some of your strips will be of medium length (18 - 24-inches). Some of the strips will be the entire width of your fabric (WOF) which will be 39-44-inches in length. See ... not even the fabric companies follow a complete standard all the time.

To make things easier on yourself, you will stitch the short pieces together into strips sets as shown. They will not all be the same length so you will do your best to make them work together. Of course, the medium pieces will all be stitched together and the long pieces together to create long strip sets. When these strip sets are cut into block sizes, they will become the same size and you will be able to stitch them together.

strip set stitched together

Be sure to read the instructions at the beginning of each pattern. Each block requires a certain width of strip set to cut the blocks. It doesn't take as many pieces sewn together to make a block as it may sometimes appear. You might be surprised how quickly your pieces are completed. I know that I was. I was also surprised at the number of quilts I was able to make from my scrap baskets without even making a dent. Keep that in mind the next time someone desperately wants a charity project. You have plenty of fabrics for creating quick and easy projects just lying around in those baskets waiting to be tamed.

Dealing With Uneven Pieces and Wonky Troublemakers

I came up with this idea from looking at antique quilts. Have you ever really looked at antiques? We see them in magazines, museums and quilt shows. Some of us purchase them for hundreds or thousands of dollars. We use them as ideas for creating our designs and even imitate and reproduce their fabrics. If you look at them really closely, you will often notice that they are far from perfect. They were made from scraps. Little pieces of leftovers. Antique string quilts (similar to *From Strips to Squares*) have seams that don't even meet, yet we love them anyway. They make interesting designs and have interesting fabrics. They are made of memories. They are made of leftovers; the things found lying around at the end of the day. Just like the fabrics in your scrap basket. These little pieces are your antiques (or they will be someday) and it's OK to put them together and make something beautiful and useful that is not quite perfect.

So, you now have all your scraps into piles to be strip pieced together and you're not quite sure what to do next. They are wrinkled and gnarled and some of them started out as 3-inch strips and make a wrong turn into 2 ¼-inches and then wobble back to 3 ¾-inches. How can you think about sewing these pieces together? They aren't even and getting them even would require you to press them nicely, attempt to fold them properly and line them up on a straight edge.

Don't do it. It isn't necessary. I know this doesn't follow the rules of any class you have ever taken or any book written, but I promise you that you can still sew them together. Lay the pieces right sides together as even as posiible, and just stitch. Pull the fabrics taut and don't worry about the wrinkles. The strips will wave a little … but it really doesn't matter. It's a scrap quilt. It's supposed to look like that. We will cut them into precise blocks later. If you leaf through the pages of this book and look at the designs you will see that the way the fabrics wiggle around really doesn't matter and adds character to the patterns. So stitch them together with reckless abandon.

Here are the rules that you should follow while piecing your strips:

- Make sure that you use at least a ¼-inch seam allowance when piecing your strips. You will be using the standard ¼-inch seam when piecing all the blocks as always but sometimes when you are piecing your strips you will find that in the middle of the piecing you run into a frayed spot and need to "take a bigger bite" out of the fabric to accommodate the variances in width. You can feel comfortable doing this because, again, the blocks will be cut to size after the strip piecing. It's more important that your seams stay together and the fabrics don't fray up to the seams.

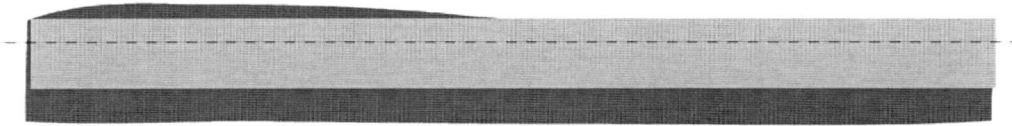

- You should press your seams after every two to three strips. If you are a pressing genius, then you will be fine following what ever rule you like. In general, fabrics can start to "accordion" after three or more strips. It is not necessary to press your seams in any certain direction but if you prefer to do it that way go right ahead. I do prefer to press with starch. I feel this helps to keep the pieces nice and flat during cutting. Don't get concerned if your strips set begin to wobble and curve in another direction. This can happen when using pieces that are uneven. Try to make sure that your strip sets are pressed nicely. This will make the cutting process more accurate.
- The more fabric variation the better. Scrap quilts look best with many different fabrics, even if they are the same color tone. If some of your strips are wider than the others you can lay them on the cutting table and use a straight edge to trim them down. They DO NOT need to be a particular measurement so getting them "even" is not necessary. Just lay them down and cut them smaller (in half or thirds) and toss the remaining strips back into the pile for the next strip set.

Scrap basket dumped on the cutting table.

Cutting Your Strip Sets Into Actual Blocks

Now that your strip sets are complete you can cut them into the necessary blocks for your chosen pattern. In some cases, you will be sewing together large triangles. They should be large enough that they won't give you any problems. Remember that you can always trim them and square them up when you are done because there are no points to cut off so don't worry if you think those pesky triangles will give you any trouble.

You will lay your ruler down on the strip sets as shown and cut out your pieces depending on the pattern you choose to make. If you own the triangle ruler or diamond ruler mentioned earlier, and it's the correct size for the blocks you want to make, then you will be able to cut directly around the ruler and flip the ruler back and forth along the length of the strip until you can't cut anymore. You can save all the leftover ends if you like. Some may be able to be used in other patterns in the book. In *Scrap Crazy* the quilt is made entirely of leftover ends of the strips sets, extra small pieces in my scrap baskets and small leftover blocks or pieces of blocks that I made for other quilts. Each pattern indicates which shape and size to cut your pieces as well as how wide your strip sets should be before you begin cutting. However, if you are using a different ruler or different size ruler, you will need to make the necessary adjustments to your quilt blocks and fabric requirements.

At times, you will find that your strip sets will curl a little and not be completely straight. This is fine. They will be plenty wide enough to accommodate your pieces. You may find that you must shift your ruler around a little to make it fit. For instance, normally when cutting triangles out of a strip you would line the ruler up with the bottom edge of the strip and cut on both sides. Then take the ruler and flip and cut the next piece and so on. In the case of these pieces your strip sets will be a little larger than the width of your pieces. You will be able to flip the ruler back and forth to some degree but always realigning within the strip set to make sure the entire shape can be cut out properly.

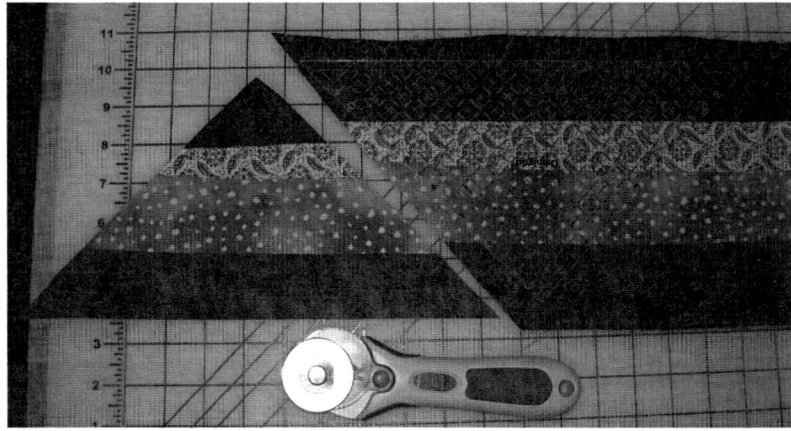

Flipping the triangle ruler on your strip set

How Not to Cut Your Hand Off

I have made a few assumptions in this book. After all, this is a book about using your scraps and so it could be assumed that you have made a few quilts in your time and have collected quite a few scraps. So I will also assume that you have learned rotary cutting safety. I know it's bad to assume, but I don't want to be responsible for imparting incorrect wisdom on the proper way to handle a rotary cutter.

On this subject, I really only have two things to say.
- Never use the rotary cutter in such a way that you are pushing towards your body or body parts. I know that some of us refuse to believe that we cannot cut in more than one direction. I admit that I have been guilty at times of using a rotary cutter improperly ... but even I have limits. You CAN pick up your pieces and turn them so that they are facing a safe cutting direction. When using the rulers, I often will cut two sides and then turn the project so that I can safely cut the third or fourth side. It is completely OK to lift and move your pieces.
- If you refuse to listen to the first direction and cut towards your hand or body please invest in a Kevlar™ glove or something out of chain mail to prevent your loss of digits.

In all seriousness, please use extreme caution when cutting these pieces. I know that while making the quilts, I was excited and was in a big hurry to cut the pieces and put them up on the design wall. I may have, at times, rushed the cutting process just a little bit. That can be a very dangerous business. It only takes another minute to pick the pieces up and turn them on your cutting table so that you can safely cut them at a better angle. If you are one of those super quilters who is capable of cutting at any angle and you choose to go your own way, that's fine. I respect that ... and I applaud you for your ability (which I can still do because both of my hands are still attached). Please be careful and have fun.

Quilt Pattern Fabric Requirements

You will notice that the patterns give no real instruction for how much fabric to buy. I do give fabric requirements for border fabrics and supplementals (all the extra things that you need). For the scrap blocks, I only give you the number of finished cut pieces and not a yardage requirement. I know to some of you it may seem as though I am not giving enough information about fabric requirements. I assure you that you will need far fewer scraps to complete these projects than it seems. You will be able to cut quite a few blocks from each strip sets depending on the length of the strips and because I am not familiar with YOUR scraps I cannot give you exact measurements. I always seemed to have more blocks than I needed for each project.

If you reach a point that you just don't have the right colors in your scrap stash and you feel the need to supplement your scrap stash, you can make strips from your stash of regular fabrics or FQs. I would suggest cutting 2-inch strips (or something about that size) from your existing stash and adding it to your scraps. This seems to be about the right size within the blocks but anything can work. Keep in mind that using your stash for these violates what we are trying to accomplish in this book, but you have it as an option if you are not happy with your color choices.

I encourage you not to get frustrated or distracted by what seems like a lack of information. The most important thing is that you get into that scrap basket and sew. It won't be long before you have enough blocks for this quilt ... and you will have plenty more left over for a new project. So let's get stitching.

Measuring to Add the Borders to Your Quilts

I feel the need to insert this paragraph on adding borders even though you have probably already learned this. I normally add this paragraph to all my patterns just as a reminder. I felt the need to put it in the book for reference, but you can feel free to add your borders anyway that you wish. I will let you know that all measurements for border strips (which include their fabric requirements and cutting instructions) are calculated to be cut across the grain in strips. If you prefer to cut or tear your borders with the grain of the fabric you will need to adjust fabric requirements because you will need more yardage. The measurements of each quilt center are found throughout the pattern so you should be able to tell the yardage measurements that you need in inches if you decide to make your borders another way.

Before adding the borders to your quilt, measure the quilt width and length of the quilt top at the mid-point of each edge (in case the outer edges have stretched). After sewing the strips together, be sure to cut the border strips to the exact width and length of the quilt top before adding them to the quilt top. This will prevent rippling and ensure that the quilt top lays flat. If you start measuring the quilt to add the top and bottom borders first, be sure to re-measure the quilt in the opposite direction before cutting the side borders.

Terminology

WOF - Width of Fabric
FQ - Fat Quarter
Unplanned Project - Scrap project using random strips of fabric with no color or tone distinction.
Color Organized Project - Scrap project with color and tone distribution before the stitching process.

THE QUILTS

From Strips to Squares
Sample size is 43-inches x 55-inches
Pattern found on Page 25

Sunshine and Shadows
Sample size is 42-inches x 52-inches
Pattern found on Page 27

Scrap Crazy
Sample size is 35-inches x 43-inches
Pattern found on Page 30

Scrappy Pyramids
Sample size is 30-inches x 40-inches
Pattern found on Page 32

Scrappy Hexagons
Sample size is 38-inches x 38-inches
Pattern found on Page 34

Ozark Table Topper
22-inches x 25-inches
Pattern found on Page 39

Scrappy Ozark Stars
Sample size is 62-inches x 62-inches
Pattern found on Page 36

Stained Glass Lily Pads
Sample size is 50-inches x 70-inches
Pattern found on Page 41

Delectable Diamond Scraps
Sample size is 40-inches x 62-inches
Pattern found on Page 43

THE PATTERNS

From Strips to Squares
43-inches x 55-inches

Notes: For this quilt I chose to put strips together based on tone. For each color I laid the strips in piles based on how closely related their color shades were. This gives the quilt the illusion of being constructed of solid pieces. The quilt has the appearance of being constructed of batiks based on the jewel tones that I chose to use, but was actually made of a variety of cottons. The trick to this quilt was not mixing in any pastels. This quilt would also look nice with a sashing. If sashed you may be able to be a bit more liberal with the colors.

Tools Used:
#96 Omnigrid® Triangle Ruler (90° x 45° angle)

~

Scrap Blocks Needed:
48 Scrap Triangles - (4 triangles of each color tone)
12 Blocks - 11 3/8-inches square

~

Supplemental Fabric Requirements:
Border Fabric : 1 yard
        5½-inch border strips
Optional Binding : ½ yard

~

Border Cutting Instructions:
From Border Fabric:
•   Cut 5½-inches x WOF strips

Note* If you adjust the size of the quilt, you will need to adjust the Border Fabric and Binding measurements and calculate the number of fabric strips needed for the border.

Step 1: Making Your Strip Sets
Decide the scrap strips you intend to use for this project and make your horizontal strip sets. Strips should be slightly larger than 6¼-inches (the width of the #96 Omnigrid® Triangle, or if using a different ruler, larger than the width of the ruler.)

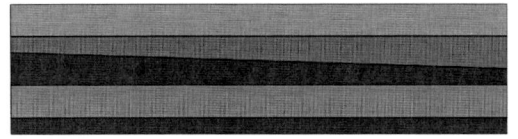

Step 2: Creating Your Blocks From Your Strip Sets
After pressing your strip sets, lay them on your cutting table and begin cutting with your triangle ruler as shown. You will be using the entire triangle so you can trim all the way around your ruler, or for safety sake, cut two sides of the angle and then lift and reposition the fabric. Square up after one or two triangles to allow for the unruly strips. Cut as many triangles from your strip sets as possible or until you reach 48.

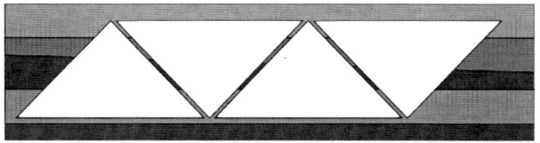

Step 3: Making the Blocks
Lay four triangles as shown in the diagram. Pick up two of the triangles, lay right sides together and stitch on the short side with ¼-inch seam. Do not worry about matching the strip seams within the triangles.
Repeat with the remaining two triangles in the block.
Layer the two units right sides together as shown, being careful to match the seams in the middle and stitch together. Repeat this process and make 12 blocks.

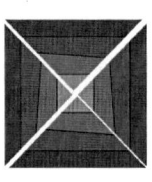

Step 4: Assembling the Quilt

Lay your blocks out in a 3 x 4 setting. Rearrange the blocks until the setting is pleasing to you. Stitch together as shown in the diagram.

Step 5: Adding the Border

I give tips in the beginning of the book about adding borders to your quilts. You may choose to change the size of this quilt so I will not give instructions on the number of strips to use.

The borders on the sample of this quilt are made from 5½-inch strips. Measure the sides of your quilt and cut the strips according to length. After attaching the strips to the sides of the quilt, re-measure the quilt for the border strips on the top and bottom of the quilt top.

Sunshine and Shadows
42-inches x 52-inches

> Notes: This quilt requires strong lights and darks to make the design work. I intentionally made a couple of "mistakes" in this one (although we both know that scrap quilts have no mistakes.) There are a couple of blocks that have darker strips in the lighter parts of the blocks. Now you know what not to do if you want to achieve this look. I was not as concerned about tones with this quilt, although the quilt has the appearance of being tonal because I put the darks with the darks and the lights with the lights. One alternative would be to use cream/white tone on tone scraps or even solid pieces of fabric to be the alternate triangles to make the pattern and use all the light and dark scraps together. That could make a very interesting quilt. This is a simple design with a simple concept so dive right in.

Tools Used:
#96 Omnigrid® Triangle Ruler (90° x 45° angle)

~

Scrap Blocks Needed:
48 Scrap Triangles - (24 light and 24 dark triangles)
These will make 12 Blocks - 11 3/8-inches square

~

Supplemental Fabric Requirements:
Border Fabric : ½ yard
          4½-inch border strips
Optional Binding : ½ yard

~

Border Cutting Instructions:
From Border Fabric:
- Cut 4½-inches x WOF strips

Note* If you adjust the size of the quilt, you will need to adjust the Border Fabric and Binding measurements and calculate the number of fabric strips needed for the border.

Step 1: Making Your Strip Sets
Decide the scrap strips you intend to use for this project and make your horizontal strip sets. Strips should be slightly larger than 6¼-inches (the width of the #96 Omnigrid® Triangle, or if using a different ruler, larger than the width of the ruler.)

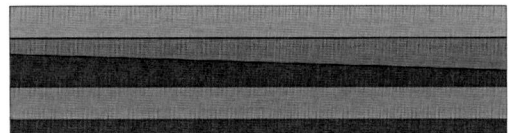

Step 2: Creating Your Blocks From Your Strip Sets
After pressing your strip sets, lay them on your cutting table and begin cutting with your triangle ruler as shown. You will be using the entire triangle so you can trim all the way around your ruler, or for safety sake, cut two sides of the angle and then lift and reposition the fabric. Square up after one or two triangles to allow for the unruly strips. Cut as many triangles from your strip sets as possible or until you reach 48.

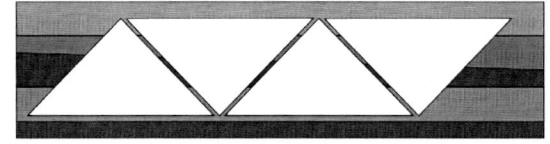

Step 3: Making the Blocks
Lay four triangles as shown in the diagram. Pick up two of the triangles, lay right sides together and stitch on the short side with ¼-inch seam. Do not worry about matching the strip seams within the triangles.

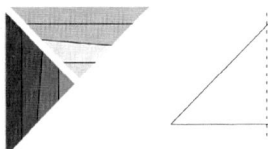

Repeat with the remaining two triangles in the block. Layer the two units right sides together as shown, being careful to match the seams in the middle and stitch together. Repeat this process and make 12 blocks.

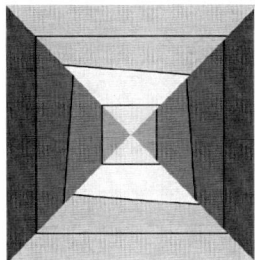

Step 4: Assembling the Quilt

Lay your blocks out in a 3 x 4 setting. Rearrange the blocks until the setting is pleasing to you. Stitch together as shown in the diagram.

Step 5: Adding the Border

I give tips in the beginning of the book about adding borders to your quilts. You may choose to change the size of this quilt so I will not give instructions on the number of strips to use.

The borders on the sample of this quilt are made from 4½-inch strips. Measure the sides of your quilt and cut the strips according to length. After attaching the strips to the sides of the quilt, re-measure the quilt for the border strips on the top and bottom of the quilt top.

Scrap Crazy
35-inches x 43-inches

Notes: I think this is the best quilt because the blocks are totally free. This quilt was made from all the leftover bits of all other quilts. I chose to use mostly reds and greens for this quilt. The colors are mixed up within some of the blocks. There are so many possibilities for this one. You can make blocks that are completely random from all your leftover bits. Sew the squares together and have a truly crazy scrappy quilt. You could sash those blocks to define their shape into squares. I love the idea of making all the blocks from different colors. You can divide them tonally also, although that would require more effort. Add in your leftover blocks or units from other quilts and create a true one-of-a-kind project. The possibilities are truly endless with this one.

Tools Used:
Standard Square Ruler

~

Scrap Blocks Needed:
12 Scrap Crazy Blocks

~

Supplemental Fabric Requirements:
Sashing Fabric : ¾ yard
Border Fabric : ¾ yard
Optional Binding : ⅓ yard

~

Border and Sashing Cutting Instructions:
From Fabric:
- Cut 5½-inches x WOF strips
- Cut 8 - 1½-inch x 7½-inch strips for sashing
- Cut 7 - 1½-inch x WOF strips for sashing

Note* If you adjust the size of the quilt, you will need to adjust the Border Fabric and Binding measurements and calculate the number of fabric strips needed for the border.

Step 1: Creating the Crazy Blocks
Using all the leftover fabric pieces from cutting your strip sets and random pieces of fabric you have lying around, start sewing fabrics together to create something resembling near a square. There really is no rhyme or reason to how these blocks go together. One option is to start with two clean cut angles leftover from some of your strip sets and stitch them together. You can trim using a straight edge on one side and then begin attaching random pieces (such as strips that were too small for your strip sets, leftover corners and such.) Rotate you block after adding each piece to make it visually interesting on all sides. Another option is to start with a block or block piece from another quilt and then build up around it on the sides.

When your mass of scraps gets bigger than 7½-inches square, take it to the cutting table and trim it to size. Repeat this process and make 12 blocks (or enough to make the size quilt you are looking for). You can cut the blocks to a larger size if you would like but I have found from experience that 7½-inches is a really nice size.

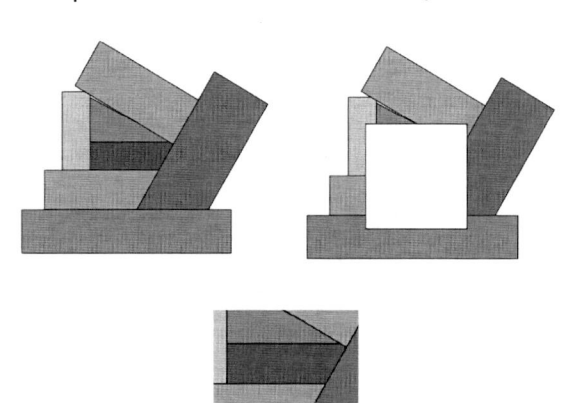

Step 2: Adding the Sashing and Assembly of Quilt

Once the blocks are in a layout that is pleasing to your eye, layer the 1½-inch x 7½-inch strips of sashing fabric vertically between each block. Stitch together as shown in the diagram to create rows.

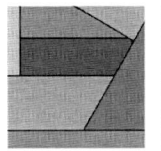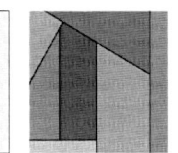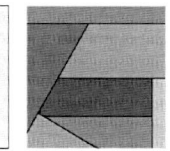

Once the rows are assembled, add the long 1½-inch strips between each row and assemble the quilt top. To ensure that the rows line up with each other, check that the seams of the rows appear to match when layering together and pin to hold in place before stitching. The rows don't to have to meet exactly but as long as they are close they will be pleasing to the eye and will appear straight.

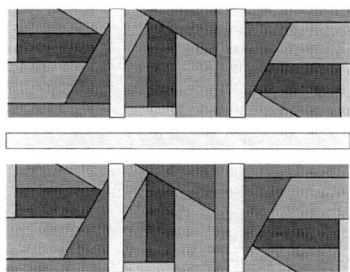

Once the top is completely assembled add the remaining sashing strips around the outside of the top as a first border, cutting the strips to the side measurements.

Step 3: Adding the Final Border

I give tips in the beginning of the book about adding borders to your quilts. You may choose to change the size of this quilt so I will not give instructions on the number of strips to use.

The borders on the sample of this quilt are made from 5½-inch strips. Measure the sides of your quilt and cut the strips according to length. After attaching the strips to the sides of the quilt, re-measure the quilt for the border strips on the top and bottom of the quilt top.

Scrappy Pyramids
30-inches x 40-inches

Tools Used:
Clearview™ 60°Triangle Ruler

~

Scrap Blocks Needed:
18 Scrap Triangles - 7-inches
17 Background Triangles - 7-inches

~

Supplemental Fabric Requirements:
Border Fabric : ½ yard
Optional Binding : ⅓ yard

~

Border Cutting Instructions:
From Border Fabric:
• Cut 4½-inches x WOF strips

Note* If you adjust the size of the quilt, you will need to adjust the Border Fabric and Binding measurements and calculate the number of fabric strips needed for the border.

Step 2: Creating Your Blocks From Your Strip Sets
After pressing your strip sets, lay them on your cutting table and begin cutting with your triangle ruler as shown. Cut two sides of the angle and then lift and reposition the fabric. Square up after one or two triangles to allow for the unruly strips. Cut as many triangles from your strip sets as possible or until you reach 18.

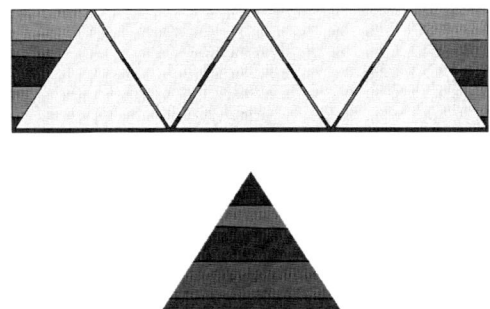

Step 1: Making Your Strip Sets
Decide the scrap strips you intend to use for this project and make your horizontal strip sets. Strips should be slightly larger than 6-inches (the height of the Clearview™ 60°Triangle Ruler, or if using a different ruler, larger than the width and height of the ruler.)

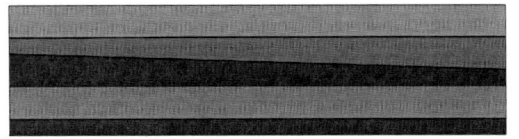

Step 3: Assembling the Quilt Top
Lay your blocks out in a setting that is pleasing to the eye with the background blocks in alternating direction. The quilt will be sewn together in rows of triangles. Triangles are sewn side to side (matching the points with no offset) and will create a nice straight edge on the top and bottom of each row.

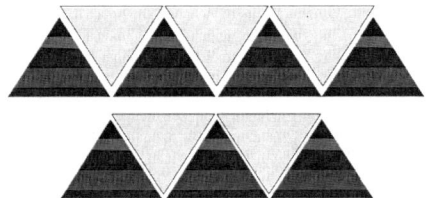

Once all the rows have been assembled, layer the rows together and carefully pin each seam so the triangle points don't shift while sewing. You will save yourself a lot of heartache if you pin your seams prior to sewing.

Step 4: Trimming the Sides of the Quilt

Once the quilt center is assembled, you will notice that the sides are not straight. You can choose to leave each point on the side of the quilt and finish the quilt with a sawtooth edge.

If you are interested in adding a border, you will need to trim the sides of the quilt straight. To do this lay the quilt top out flat on your cutting mat. Using your longest quilting ruler, lay the ruler along the side of the quilt with the ¼-inch line along the seam allowance in the blocks. Trim the side of the quilt at the ¼-inch seam allowance making certain that you do not cut off the seam allowance. This will ensure that the seam of the border falls right at the tips of the triangles. Trim both sides before adding the borders.

Step 5: Adding the Borders

I give tips in the beginning of the book about adding borders to your quilts. You may choose to change the size of this quilt so I will not give instructions on the number of strips to use.

The borders on the sample of this quilt are made from 4½-inch strips. Measure the sides of your quilt and cut the strips according to length. After attaching the strips to the sides of the quilt, re-measure the quilt for the border strips on the top and bottom of the quilt top.

Scrappy Hexagons
38-inches x 38-inches

Notes: I love making a quilt with bright colors and brown. This quilt is made with triangles again but blocks are turned to create a hexagon. I love the color spots. The blocks and strips were divided by color but use all manner of tones. Some of the hexagons are more hidden than others. This is to show you the difference between the block created in tones and just colors. The quilt size is very easily adjustable, just make more blocks. You can also make hexagons from florals as well. It all depends on your scraps and your desired outcome. Put your triangles on the design wall and see what you come up with.

Tools Used:
Clearview™ 60° Triangle Ruler

~

Scrap Blocks Needed:
66 Scrap Triangles - 6-inches
8 triangles per block.

~

Supplemental Fabric Requirements:
Border Fabric : ½ yard
Optional Binding : ⅓ yard

~

Border Cutting Instructions:
From Border Fabric:
•   Cut 3½-inches x WOF strips

Note* If you adjust the size of the quilt, you will need to adjust the Border Fabric and Binding measurements and calculate the number of fabric strips needed for the border.

Step 1: Making Your Strip Sets
Decide the scrap strips you intend to use for this project and make your horizontal strip sets. Strips should be slightly larger than 6-inches (the height of the Clearview™ 60° Triangle Ruler, or if using a different ruler, larger than the width and height of the ruler.)

Step 2: Creating Your Blocks From Your Strip Sets
After pressing your strip sets, lay them on your cutting table and begin cutting with your triangle ruler as shown. Cut two sides of the angle and then lift and reposition the fabric. Square up after one or two triangles to allow for the unruly strips. You can trim the strip to the height of the ruler if this makes cutting easier for you. Cut as many triangles from your strip sets as possible or until you reach 66.

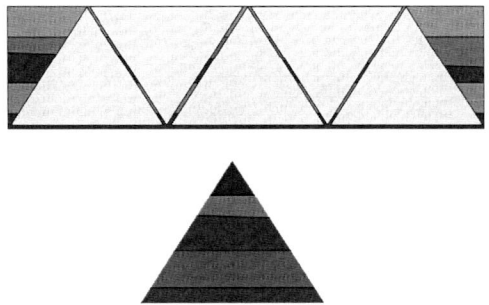

Step 3: Assembling the Quilt Top
To create the hexagon look, lay the blocks out so that the stripes within each triangle begin to make a circle (or hexagon.) Lay your blocks out in a setting that is pleasing to the eye. The quilt will be sewn together in rows of triangles. Triangles are sewn side to side (matching the points with no offset) and will create a nice straight edge on the top and bottom of each row.

Once all the rows have been assembled, layer the rows together and carefully pin each seam so the triangle points don't shift while sewing. You will save yourself a lot of heartache if you pin your seams prior to sewing.

Step 4: Trimming the Sides of the Quilt

Once the quilt center is assembled, you will notice that the sides are not straight. You can choose to leave each point on the side of the quilt and finish the quilt with a sawtooth edge.

If you are interested in adding a border, you will need to trim the sides of the quilt straight. Lay the quilt top out flat on your cutting mat. Using your longest quilting ruler, lay the ruler along the side of the quilt with the ¼-inch line along the seam allowance in the blocks. Trim the side of the quilt at the ¼-inch seam allowance making certain that you do not cut off the seam allowance. This will ensure that the seam of the border falls right at the tips of the triangles. Trim both sides before adding the borders.

Step 5: Adding the Final Border

I give tips in the beginning of the book about adding borders to your quilts. You may choose to change the size of this quilt so I will not give instructions on the number of strips to use.

The borders on the sample of this quilt are made from 3½-inch strips. Measure the sides of your quilt and cut the strips according to length. After attaching the strips to the sides of the quilt, re-measure the quilt for the border strips on the top and bottom of the quilt top.

Scrappy Ozark Stars
62-inches x 62-inches

Notes: You will notice with this quilt that I divided the scraps tonally as well as by color. One block uses a leftover floral print in the center and gold accents for the star points. It works out pretty well. You can use a different tone for the inside and outside of the star or make them all the same tone like the sample. You can also make these blocks completely scrappy. The background fabric makes the stars really stand out so it wouldn't matter what fabrics you used to make them. Changing the color of the background would change the look of the quilt dramatically. You will also notice that I ended the pattern on the sides with "arrows" rather than ½ of the star block. This was an interesting suggestion from a friend and I really love the way it turned out. You can choose to add the additional triangles and finish out the star pattern if you choose. Either way the quilt will be beautiful. A design wall will help a great deal.

Tools Used:
Clearview™ 60˚Triangle Ruler

~

Scrap Blocks Needed:
104 Scrap Triangles - 6-inches
86 Scrap Background Triangles - 6-inches

~

Supplemental Fabric Requirements:
Background Fabric : 1⅓ yards
Border Fabric : 1¼ yards
Optional Binding : ½ yard

~

Border Cutting Instructions:
From Border Fabric:
• Cut 5½-inches x WOF strips

Note* If you adjust the size of the quilt, you will need to adjust the Border Fabric and Binding measurements and calculate the number of fabric strips needed for the border.

Step 1: Making Your Strip Sets
Decide the scrap strips you intend to use for this project and make your horizontal strip sets. Strips should be slightly larger than 6-inches (the height of the Clearview™ 60˚Triangle Ruler, or if using a different ruler, larger than the width and height of the ruler.)

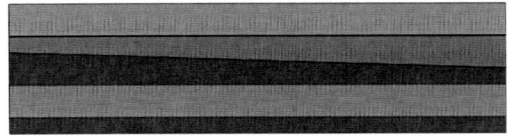

Step 2: Creating Your Blocks From Your Strip Sets
After pressing your strip sets, lay them on your cutting table and begin cutting with your triangle ruler as shown. Cut two sides of the angle and then lift and reposition the fabric. Square up after one or two triangles to allow for the unruly strips. You can trim the strip to the height of the ruler if this makes cutting easier for you. Cut as many triangles from your strip sets as possible or until you reach 104.

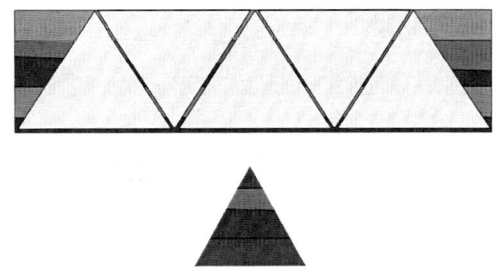

Step 3: Creating the Blocks
To create the hexagon look, lay the blocks out so that the stripes within each triangle begin to make a circle (or hexagon).

You cannot assemble the hexagons themselves together due to the way the triangles must be stitched, however, you could do a partial assembly by stitching one side (3 triangles) in the row as shown to prevent the pieces from getting mixed up.

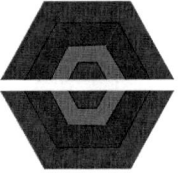

Add the points to the stars by adding another triangle to the opposing side of each flat side of the hexagon in your layout as shown in the diagram. This completes the design of the Ozark Star.   We still have not begun the assembly.

Add the background triangles to the layout with all blocks together to complete each row as show in the diagram. There will be two background triangles (giving the appearance of a diamond) between each of the stars.

When you have finished your layout in the size you like you can add the additional scrap triangles to the quilt in the arrow pattern shown to complete the design.

The quilt will be sewn together in rows of triangles. Triangles are sewn side to side (matching the points with no offset) and will create a nice straight edge on the top and bottom of each row.

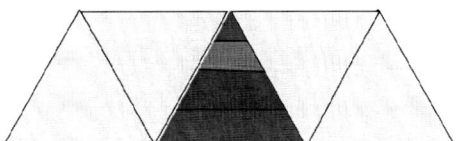

Once all the rows have been assembled, layer the rows together and carefully pin each seam so the triangle points don't shift while sewing. You will save yourself a lot of heartache if you pin your seams prior to sewing.

Step 4: Trimming the Sides of the Quilt
Once the quilt center is assembled, you will notice that the sides are not straight. You can choose to leave each point on the side of the quilt and finish the quilt with a sawtooth edge.
If you are interested in adding a border, you will need to trim the sides of the quilt straight. Lay the quilt top out flat on your cutting mat. Using your longest quilting ruler, lay the ruler along the side of the quilt with the ¼-inch line along the seam allowance in the blocks. Trim the side of the quilt at the ¼-inch seam allowance making certain that you do not cut off the seam allowance. This will ensure that the seam of the border falls right at the tips of the triangles. Trim both sides before adding the borders.

Step 5: Adding the Final Border

I give tips in the beginning of the book about adding borders to your quilts. You may choose to change the size of this quilt so I will not give instructions on the number of strips to use.

The borders on the sample of this quilt are made from 3½-inch strips. Measure the sides of your quilt and cut the strips according to length. After attaching the strips to the sides of the quilt, re-measure the quilt for the border strips on the top and bottom of the quilt top.

Ozark Table Topper
22-inches x 25-inches

Notes: This is a great little table topper made with one of the blocks from the quilt. I chose to mix the colors within the whole star. Yours can be made any numbers of ways: completely scrappy, one color in the middle and another color around the outside, all one color... any way you choose. You may also add a border to make it fit your table.

Tools Used:
Clearview™ 60°Triangle Ruler

~

Scrap Blocks Needed:
12 Scrap Triangles - 6-inches
12 Scrap Background Triangles - 6-inches

~

Supplemental Fabric Requirements:
Optional Border Fabric for 2½-inch border : ¼ yard
Optional Binding for Topper without border : ¼ yard

~

Note* If you adjust the size of the quilt, you will need to adjust the Border Fabric and Binding measurements and calculate the number of fabric strips needed for the border.

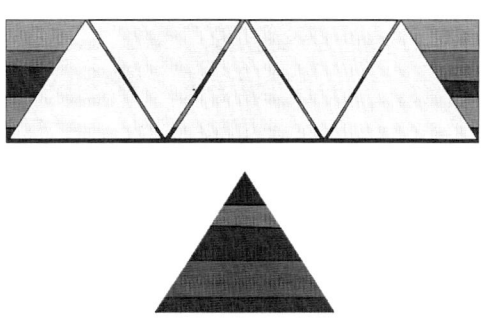

Step 3: Creating the Blocks
To create the hexagon, look lay the blocks out so that the stripes within each triangle begin to make a circle (or hexagon) as shown in the diagram.

You cannot assemble the hexagons themselves together due to the way the triangles must be stitched, however, you could doa partial assembly by stitching one side (3 triangles) in the row as shown to prevent the pieces from getting mixed up.

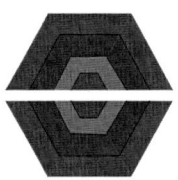

Add the points to the stars by adding another triangle to the opposing side of each flat side of the hexagon in your layout as shown in the diagram. This completes the design of the Ozark Star. We still have not begun the assembly.

Step 1: Making Your Strip Sets
Decide the scrap strips you intend to use for this project and make your horizontal strip sets. Strips should be slightly larger than 6-inches (the height of the Clearview™ 60°Triangle Ruler, or if using a different ruler, larger than the width and height of the ruler.)

Step 2: Creating Your Blocks From Your Strip Sets
After pressing your strip sets, lay them on your cutting table and begin cutting with your triangle ruler as shown. Cut two sides of the angle and then lift and reposition the fabric. Square up after one or two triangles to allow for the unruly strips. You can trim the strip to the height of the ruler if this makes cutting easier for you. Cut as many triangles from your strip sets as possible or until you reach 12.

Add the background triangles to the layout with all blocks together to complete each row as show in the diagram.

Lay your blocks out in a setting that is pleasing to the eye. The quilt will be sewn together in rows of triangles. Triangles are sewn side to side (matching the points with no offset) and will create a nice straight edge on the top and bottom of each row.

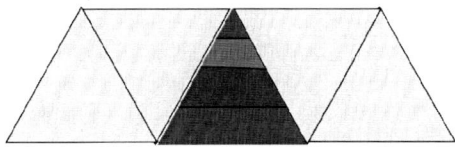

Once all the rows have been assembled, layer the rows together and carefully pin each seam so the triangle points don't shift while sewing. You will save yourself a lot of heartache if you pin your seams prior to sewing.

Step 4: Finishing the Project
Your project is now ready to be quilted and bound. You can add a border to the project if you wish to make your project larger.

I give tips in the beginning of the book about adding borders to your quilts. You may choose to change the size of this quilt so I will not give instructions on the number of strips to use.

EXTRA NOTE:

If you are interested in adding a border to this project, don't be discouraged by its shape. Adding a border to a hexagon is very easy. You will simply add your border strips to opposite sides of the project (2 sides at a time) and then trim the next sides with a straight. Below are diagrams that may help illustrate this technique. You will continue adding the border to the two opposing sides until you are all the way around the hexagon. Trim each side of the hexagon when complete.

Stained Glass Lily Pads
50-inches x 70-inches

Notes: This quilt started out as a hexagon quilt with a black background and the suggestion was made that I show two quilts in one. At one end of the quilt you will notice that the "lily pads" are all connected directly with the single black background triangles. If you wanted a symmetrical quilt this would be the way you would lay the quilt out. The other end of the quilt shows the "lily pads" floating away from the rest of the group (some floated right into the border). The idea is that you can put your quilt together any way you like. You could add more space to the blocks and shift them so they appear to be assembled in a zig-zag pattern. Also changing the background makes a completely different look. The blocks on the sample read as a solid but could be completely scrappy as well. Adding the blocks to the border is very simple but you can just put a plain border on your quilt if that's what you choose. The idea for the name comes from the quilting.

Tools Used:
Clearview™ 60° Triangle Ruler

~

Scrap Blocks Needed:
66 Scrap Triangles - 6-inches
    11 hexagon blocks for this quilt.
73 Background Triangles - 6-inches

~

Supplemental Fabric Requirements:
Border Fabric : 1⅓ yard
Optional Binding : ½ yard

~

Border Cutting Instructions:
From Border Fabric:
- Cut 4 - 6½-inches x WOF strips
- Cut 4 - 1½-inches x WOF strips
- Cut 4 - 7½-inches x WOF strips

Note* If you adjust the size of the quilt, you will need to adjust the Border Fabric and Binding measurements and calculate the number of fabric strips needed for the border.

Step 1: Making Your Strip Sets
Decide the scrap strips you intend to use for this project and make your horizontal strip sets. Strips should be slightly larger than 6-inches (the height of the Clearview™ 60° Triangle Ruler, or if using a different ruler, larger than the width and height of the ruler.)

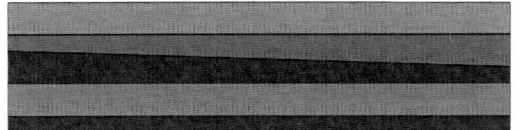

Step 2: Creating Your Blocks From Your Strip Sets
After pressing your strip sets, lay them on your cutting table and begin cutting with your triangle ruler as shown. Cut two sides of the angle and then lift and reposition the fabric. Square up after one or two triangles to allow for the unruly strips. You can trim the strip to the height of the ruler if this makes cutting easier for you. Cut as many triangles from your strip sets as possible or until you reach 66.

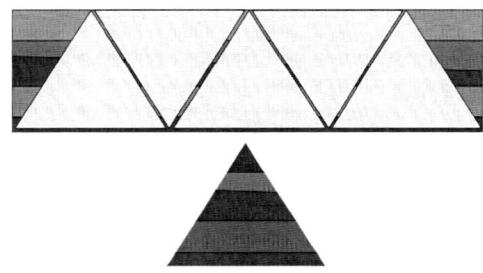

Step 3: Creating the Blocks
To create the hexagon look, lay the blocks out so that the stripes within each triangle begin to make a circle (or hexagon).

You cannot assemble the hexagons themselves together due to the way the triangles must be stitched, however, you could do a partial assembly by stitching one side (3 triangles) in the row as shown to prevent the pieces from getting mixed up.

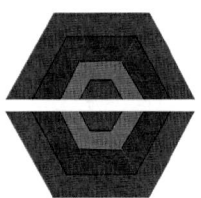

This quilt layout came about from a lot of playing with the blocks on the design wall. As you move your hexagons around, put more background triangles in and make a layout that is pleasing to you.

The quilt will be sewn together in vertical rows of triangles. Triangles are sewn side to side (matching the points with no offset) and will create a nice straight edge on the top and bottom of each row.

Once all the rows have been assembled, layer the rows together and carefully pin each seam so the triangle points don't shift while sewing. You will save yourself a lot of heartache if you pin your seams prior to sewing.

If you are making your quilt exactly like the pattern, you will have two hexagons stretching into the border of the quilt. The half hexagons that are going into the border will be attached along with the border piece. So leave the 2 outer pieces off of the quilt top until the border is assembled.

Step 4: Trimming the Sides of the Quilt

To make the quilt the same as the pattern you must trim the quilt top and bottom. Lay the quilt top out flat on your cutting mat. Using your longest quilting ruler, lay the ruler along the side of the quilt with the ¼-inch line along the seam allowance in the blocks. Trim the top and bottom of the quilt at the ¼-inch seam allowance making certain that you do not cut off the seam allowance. This will ensure that the seam of the border falls right at the tips of the triangles. Trim both sides of the quilt with the overhanging blocks.

Step 5: Adding the Final Border

In order for the two hexagons on the edge of the quilt to appear they are hanging out in the border you must cut the border strips to sew around them. Lay the border strip on your cutting table and take the 60° Triangle Ruler and trim the edge in the direction that matches the block edge as shown in the diagram below. This will create a border piece that will sew the edge of the hexagon to the edge of the quilt top.

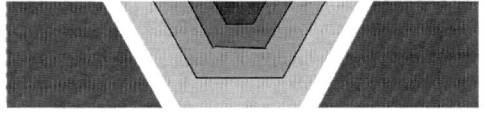

Sew the border piece to the ½ hexagon, making sure that you are attaching to the correct side in the correct direction. Note that one of the sides of the border will be much shorter than the other since the hexagons is attached to the far end of the quilt top.

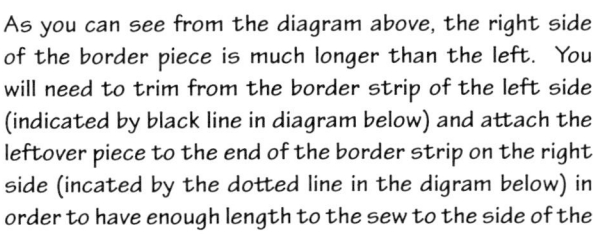

As you can see from the diagram above, the right side of the border piece is much longer than the left. You will need to trim from the border strip of the left side (indicated by black line in diagram below) and attach the leftover piece to the end of the border strip on the right side (incated by the dotted line in the digram below) in order to have enough length to the sew to the side of the quilt.

Once the long border strip, with the ½ hexagon in it, is stitched together you will attach it to the side of the quilt. Be sure to pin the hexagon pieces together so that they match and stitch the border on the side of the quilt. Sewed the border piece on, then press and trim the quilt top square

You will repeat this process on the other side of the quilt with the remaining ½ hexagon on the opposite side using the same method.

Then using the method for adding border strips, you will add the 1½-inch border strips onto both sides of the quilt top outside of the borders with the hexagons. This gives the quilt the appearance of having the hexagons laying inside the border but not to the edge.

The borders on the top and bottom of this quilt are made from 7½-inch strips. Measure the width of your quilt and cut the strips according to length and add to top and bottom of the quilt top.

Delectable Diamond Scraps
40-inches x 62-inches

Notes: This quilt began with some scraps of a leftover floral border print. It is completely scrappy as I added fabrics whose tones do not exist within the border print. I did use two or three different florals and alternate their position in the diamonds. You can piece fabrics for your small diamonds but I chose to cut the diamonds from scraps that were 3½-inches or larger so that they would be solid. After assembling the smaller diamonds into larger blocks, I then measured the blocks to determine the size of the background blocks. You can make your quilt entirely of scraps or use tone-on-tone scraps for the background diamonds. There are lots of possibilities to use what you have. Concentrate on keeping your points meeting in the middle of the top... don't worry about cutting of the points on the tops and sides of the quilt.

Tools Used:
Fussy Cutter™ Ruler Set 45° Diamond

~

Scrap Blocks Needed:
80 Scrap Diamonds - 3-inches
30 Background Diamonds - 5½-inches
(make sure to measure your blocks to check this size)

~

Supplemental Fabric Requirements:
Border Fabric : 1¼ yards
Optional Binding : ½ yard

~

Border Cutting Instructions:
From Border Fabric:
• Cut 6½-inches x WOF strips

Note* If you adjust the size of the quilt, you will need to adjust the Border Fabric and Binding measurements and calculate the number of fabric strips needed for the border.

Step 1: Cutting Your Diamond Blocks
The blocks in this quilt were cut from scrap strips that were 3-inches or more in width. Lay your strips on your cutting table and begin cutting with your diamond ruler as shown. Cut the angle and then lift and reposition the ruler. Square up after one or two diamonds if need be to allow for the unruly strips. Cut as many triangles from your strip sets as possible or until you reach 80. If need be you can piece strip sets and cut scrappy diamonds as shown below.

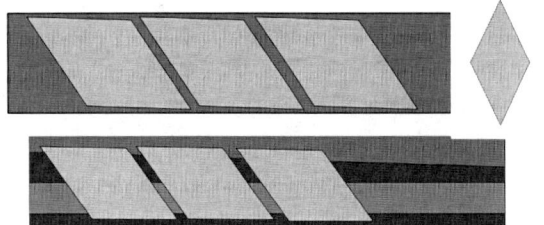

Step 2: Creating the Blocks
Lay your scrap diamonds out together on a design wall and arrange the pieces into four patch diamonds as shown in the diagram. After the diamonds are arranged into sets that are pleasing to you it is time to sew them together. Each block will be sew in a diagonal setting. Diamonds must be offset ¼-inch to allow for seams. Please be sure to see the alignment diagram for your diamonds before sewing or you will sew them incorrectly.

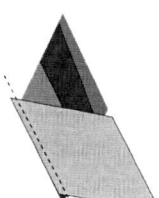

In this pattern I used a floral print and alternated the floral print in two different block layouts as shown. You will need 10 of each block layout shown to complete the quilt.

Repeat this process and stitch together all of your four patch diamond blocks. You will then measure the blocks to check the size before cutting your background diamonds. Once the blocks have been measured, cut out the background diamonds and use your design wall to arrange all the blocks as shown in the diagram.

Step 3: Assembly of the Quilt

Referring to the quilt diagram, and after the blocks have been arranged, begin sewing the blocks in diagonal rows. In a diagonal setting, the blocks and setting triangles are sewn together from the corner of the quilt top as shown in the diagram. Diamonds must be offset ¼-inch to allow for seams. Please be sure to refer to the alignment diagram for your diamonds in STEP 3 before sewing or you will sew them incorrectly.

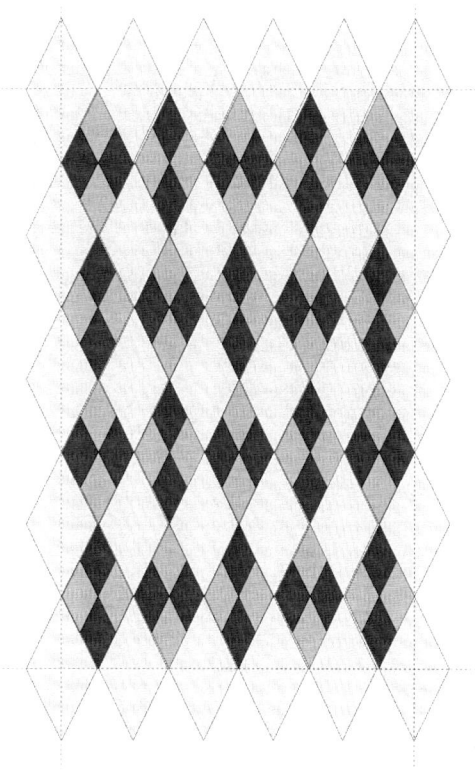

Step 4: Trimming the Sides of the Quilt

Once the quilt center is assembled, you will notice that the sides are not straight. You can choose to leave each point on the side of the quilt and finish the quilt with a sawtooth edge.

If you are interested in adding a border, you will need to trim the sides of the quilt straight. Lay the quilt top out flat on your cutting mat. Using your longest quilting ruler, lay the ruler along the side of the quilt with the ¼-inch line along the seam allowance in the blocks. Trim the side of the quilt at the ¼-inch seam allowance making certain that you do not cut off the seam allowance. This will ensure that the seam of the border falls right at the tips of the triangles. Trim all the sides before adding the borders (as shown in the top right diagram.)

Step 5: Adding the Borders

I give tips in the beginning of the book about adding borders to your quilts. You may choose to change the size of this quilt so I will not give instructions on the number of strips to use.

The borders on the sample of this quilt are made from 6½-inch strips. Measure the top and bottom of your quilt and cut the strips according to length. After attaching the strips to the sides of the quilt, re-measure the quilt for the border strips on the sides of the quilt top.

If you enjoyed this book please check out one of the other titles available from Cabin In The Woods Quilters.

All Scrapped Out!
A guide to making a masterpiece from
your unruly collection of scraps.
© March 2011

Civil War Sampler
Block of the Month
© January 2009

Check the website for new releases.
New titles coming in 2013.
www.cabininthewoodsquilters.com

ABOUT THE AUTHOR

Penni Domikis is the owner of Cabin in the Woods Quilters, a quilt pattern design company established in 2003. A self-proclaimed Jill-of-all-trades, Penni was introduced to quilting by a family friend and combined her love of this new hobby, along with her passions for photography and graphic design, into a thriving pattern design business. As an award-winning quilter, Penni has developed a reputation for breaking down quilt designs into manageable pieces for quilters of all skill levels, following her company's motto, "Make it simple ... but make it with style!" She loves the creativity of coming up with new designs and delights in all aspects of the pattern process, from the cutting, to the stitching, to the print layout for production. She loves meeting quilters all over the country at classes, workshops and quilt shows and enjoys seeing her designs stitched and recreated by other quilters. Penni houses her office and design studio in the log cabin lovingly reconstructed by her husband after its catastrophic loss to fire in 1999. Penni's home and wooded surroundings lend more than a name to Cabin In The Woods Quilters. The beauty of the surrounding nature provide her with continual inspiration while allowing the freedom and flexibility to spend more time being a mom. Penni resides in Fredericksburg, Virginia and shares her home with her husband, three sons and three dogs.